Listening with Love
Foundations of Pastoral Care

Rev. Marti Steiner Unger
Rev. Dr. John R. Unger II

Come to me, all you that are weary and are carrying heavy burdens and I will give you rest. Take my yoke upon you and learn from me; for I am gentle and humble in heart, and you will find rest for your souls, for my yoke is easy, and my burden is light.
Matthew 11: 28-30

Dear Faith Leader,

As faith leaders (both clergy and laity), we are called to embody the love and compassion of Christ in all we do, especially in caring for those who are hurting and in need. The Apostle Paul reminds us, "Praise be to the God and Father of our Lord Jesus Christ, the Father of compassion and the God of all comfort, who comforts us in all our troubles, so that we can comfort those in any trouble with the comfort we ourselves receive from God" (2 Corinthian 1:3-4). It is in this spirit that we are excited to introduce "Listening with Love: Foundations of Pastoral Care."

Listening with Love is designed to equip faith leaders with practical skills and perspectives to provide Christ centered, compassionate, effective pastoral care *with* those in congregations and communities who are struggling: from trauma, health issues, mental illness, loss, financial issues, addiction… whatever is causing distress. Jesus himself modeled the utmost compassion for the brokenhearted, the outcast, and the afflicted. He listened without judgment, offered hope and healing, and always pointed people to God's unfailing love. As his disciples, we too must learn to listen with love – with genuine empathy, patience, and grace.

Through this training, you will:

- Gain biblical foundations for a compassionate, non-judgmental approach to pastoral care.
- Develop active listening skills to engage empathetically and guide others to their own solutions.
- Practice motivational interviewing techniques to help others navigate challenges and changes in their lives.
- Describe the impact of bias and stigma that can be common barriers to providing effective pastoral care.
- Learn to incorporate centering prayer to connect with God and to divine guidance in caregiving relationships while acknowledging pastoral caregivers' own need for spiritual renewal.

Imagine the transformation in your church and community as you and your ministry leaders gain competence and confidence in providing pastoral care. Envision the unique opportunity to embody the compassionate and restorative love of Christ, The Great Shepherd, by providing hope and support for healing and transformation of individuals and communities.

We invite you to join us for this transformational training to grow in the life-changing ministry of pastoral care. As we learn together to listen with the love of Christ, may we see God's kingdom come and his will be done in and through the lives of those we serve.

In Christ's love,

The Rev. Marti Steiner Unger
The Rev. Dr. John R. Unger II

In the same way, let your light shine before others, so that they may see your good works and give glory to your Father in heaven.

Matthew 5:16

Introductions

Please take a moment and write the three most important things in your life.

Example: Family, friends, career, school, faith, pets, etc…

1.

2.

3.

Next, you will have five minutes to introduce yourself to a classmate by sharing why you chose the three things most important to you in your introduction. The person listening will need to consider the three things of the person being interviewed. Each participant will have five minutes- we will let you know when it is time to switch.

Take a moment to reflect.

How did this exercise make you feel?

_____

_____

_____

_____

_____

_____

_____

The Spectrum of Attitudes

In the *Technology of Prevention Workbook*, William A. Loftquist developed the three spectrums of attitudes—people viewed as objects, people viewed as recipients and people viewed as resources. Let's explore the meaning of the spectrum of attitudes, and how it is relevant to pastoral care.

People Viewed as Objects – Do _TO_

This attitude is when a person or group of people "know what's best" for another person or group of people. The person or group of people does programs and activities TO another person or group of people (it is when we "should" on people).

Reflection: When were you treated as an object and how did you feel?

_____

_____

_____

_____

People Viewed as Recipients – Do _FOR_

This attitude is when a person or group of people still believes they "know what's best for the other person or group of people, but they "give" them the opportunity in some decision making, thinking it will be "good" for them. The person or group of people does programs and activities FOR another person or group of people.

Reflection: When were you treated as a recipient and how did you feel?

_____

_____

_____

_____

_____

_____

People Viewed as Resources – Do _WITH_

This attitude is when a person or group of people has respect for another person or group of people on what can be done. This attitude promotes self-esteem and productivity. The person or group of people does programs and activities _WITH_ another person or group of people.

Reflection: When were you treated as a resource and how did you feel?

_____

_____

_____

_____

_____

_____

_____

The attitude of WITH creates a community in which people are viewed, respected, and involved as resources is the goal of someone providing pastoral care by listening with love. The focus is on building relationships where people are treated as resources, knowing that they are valued as they are and able to overcome challenges they are facing.

"We have gifts that differ according to the grace given to us:
prophecy, in proportion to faith;
ministry, in ministering;
the teacher, in teaching;
the encourager, in encouragement;
the giver, in sincerity;
the leader, in diligence;
the compassionate, in cheerfulness."

Romans 12;6-8

Looking Inward

Please put a + beside three groups of people you would *prefer* to offer pastoral care to and a − beside three groups of people you would *prefer not* to offer pastoral care to.

We will *NOT* be sharing these.

Someone with multiple piercings
Someone who identifies as Hispanic
Someone who is incarcerated
Someone who is over 65 years old
Women
Someone who is wealthy
Someone who identifies as gay/lesbian
Someone who identifies as Muslim
Someone who struggles with an opioid
   addiction
Someone who identifies as Christian
Someone who is in a wheelchair
Someone who is under 25 years old
Someone who identifies as transgender
Someone who is black
Someone who identifies as atheist
Someone who is housing challenged
Someone who is obese

Someone with tattoos
Someone who identifies as Asian
Someone who's political affiliation is
   not yours
Someone who is a convicted drug
   dealer
Someone who identifies as white
Someone who identifies as queer
Someone who is a single parent
Someone with a mental health issue
Someone in a powerful position
Someone who is a convicted pedophile
Men
Someone who fidgets
Someone with strong perfume
Someone who identifies as Native
   American
Someone with poor hygiene
Someone with green hair

Bias

"For God so loved the world that he gave his only Son, so that everyone who believes in him may not perish but may have eternal life. Indeed, God did not send the Son into the world to condemn the world but in order that the world might be saved through him."

According to *Marriam-Webster* (n.d.), "bias" is defined as "a personal and sometimes unreasoned judgment: prejudice."

> A bias is a tendency, inclination, or prejudice toward or against something or someone. Some biases are positive and helpful—like choosing to only eat foods that are considered healthy or staying away from someone who has knowingly caused harm. But biases are often based on stereotypes, rather than actual knowledge of an individual or circumstance. Whether positive or negative, such cognitive shortcuts can result in prejudgments that lead to rash decisions or discriminatory practices. (*Psychology Today*, 2020, para. 1)

As people providing pastoral care, we need to be aware of our biases, so that we can treat the person we are listening to respectfully and fairly. If we realize we are experiencing projecting bias, we can reflect on why we are feeling that way and consider how to overcome the bias.

How might we overcome our own biases?

_____

_____

_____

_____

_____

"Teacher, which commandment in the law is the greatest?"

He said to him,

"You shall love the Lord your God with all your heart, and with all your soul, and with all your mind.'

This is the greatest and first commandment. And a second is like it:

'You shall love your neighbor as yourself.'

On these two commandments hang all the law and the prophets."

Matthew 22:36-40

Reflection:

How did this exercise make you feel? Why do we do this exercise in class?

_____

_____

_____

_____

_____

_____

_____

_____

_____

_____

_____

_____

_____

_____

_____

_____

_____

_____

_____

_____

_____

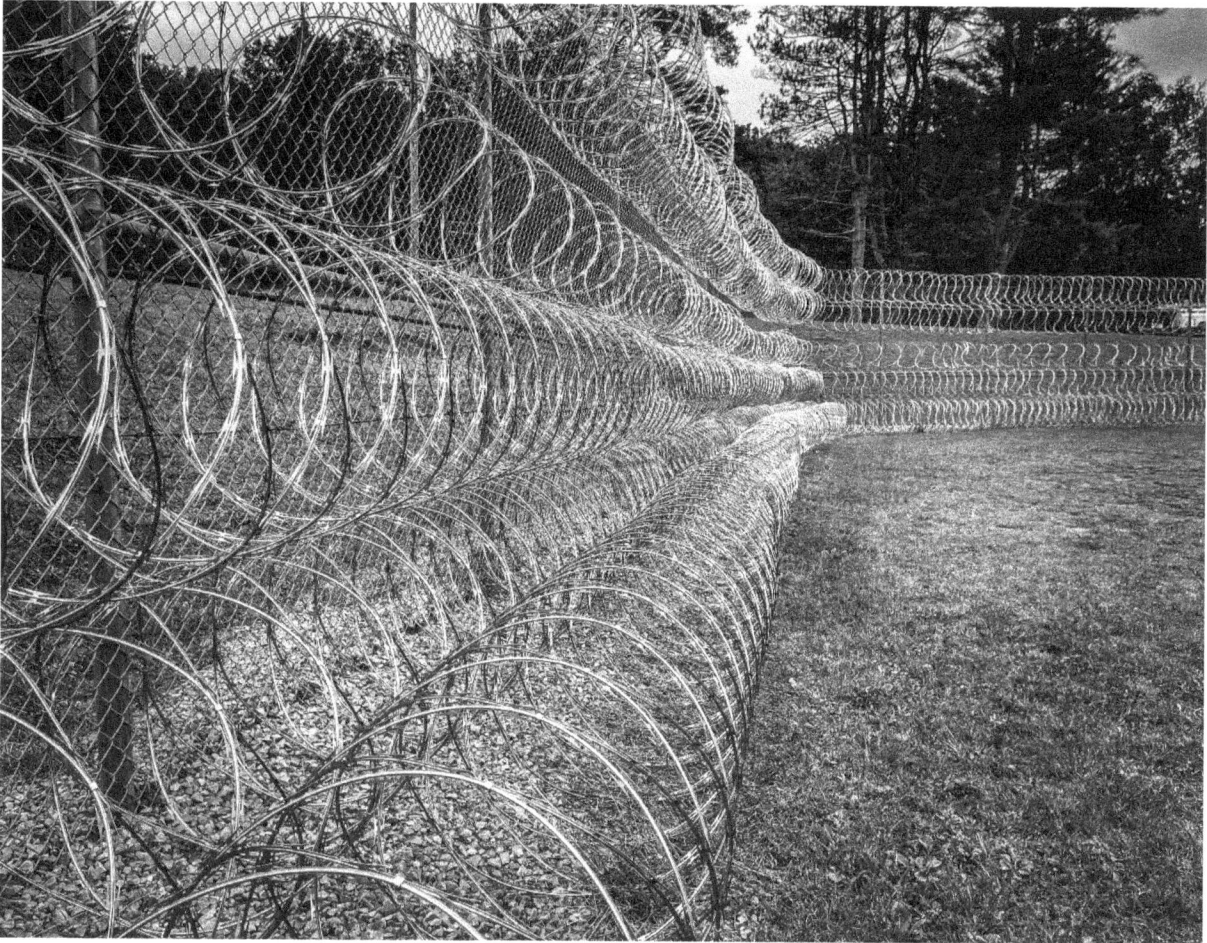

Do not judge, so that you may not be judged.

For the judgment you give will be the judgment you get,

and the measure you give will be the measure you get.

Matthew 7:1-2

Stigma

According to the Merriam-Webster (n.d.) dictionary, the definition of stigma is:

a mark of shame or discredit [--]

Stigma was borrowed from Latin stigmat-, stigma, meaning "mark, brand," and comes from Greek stizein, meaning "to tattoo." Stigma in English first referred to a scar left by a hot iron—that is, a brand. In modern use the scar is figurative: stigma most often refers to a set of negative and often unfair beliefs that a society or group of people have about something—for example, people talk about the stigma associated with mental illness, or the stigma of poverty. (Paras. 1 & 10)

Greenstein (2017) stresses that "stigma causes people to feel ashamed for something that *is* out of their control. Worst of all, stigma prevents people from seeking the help they need."

"Stigma can negatively affect the emotional, mental, and physical health of stigmatized groups and the communities they live in. Stigmatized individuals may experience isolation, depression, anxiety, or public embarrassment. Stopping stigma is important to making *all* communities and community members safer and healthier" (*CDC*, 2020, para. 17).

According to William White, our lives are greatly impacted by the words we use about ourselves and others. The words we choose to use to describe people can:

empower or disempower,

humanize or objectify,

engender compassion or elicit fear and hatred,

inspire us or deflate us,

comfort us or wound us,

bring us together or render us enemies. (p. 2)

How can we help people 'CLEAR' stigma?

CLEAR Stigma

Here is an acronym to help us work together to 'CLEAR' stigma.

Compassion- Listen with an open heart. Nurture your relationship by showing kindness and humility without judgement.

Language- In the last exercise, we saw examples of language that was not helpful to people who are stigmatized. Perhaps this was even language we ourselves have used before. How can we change our language to reduce stigma? How can we educate others to use better language?

Use language that empowers people.

Empowerment- Explore and encourage the discovery of solutions to issues the person dealing with. Don't tell them what to do, as we *do not know* exactly what they have experienced, nor do we know what a good pathway to betterment will be. Instead, help them discover their own path!

Affirmation- Encourage the person you are providing pastoral care to!

Respect- Be curious, present and demonstrate respect through your actions. Thank them for the opportunity to walk with them as they grow with God.

CLEARING stigma is important for all people…

it is how we put the human back into humanity.

"If one gives answer before hearing, it is his folly and shame."

Proverbs 18:13

Active Listening

What is active listening?

Active listening is the ability to focus completely on the person sharing, to try to understand where they are coming from and comprehend their feelings and respond thoughtfully.

People providing pastoral care are active listeners. Active listeners use verbal and non-verbal techniques to show empathy and keep attention on the person sharing. It is important for the person sharing to see that the person providing pastoral care is focused and engaged in what they have to say. Active listening builds connection, mutual trust and helps the person sharing identify and find solutions to issues faced.

People don't care how much you know, until they know how much you care!

Active listening skills: Verbal

Display empathy - The person sharing must recognize the person providing pastoral care is able to recognize their emotions and share their feelings. By showing empathy, the pastoral care provider can connect with the sharer and begin establishing trust.

> **Example:** *"I am so sorry you are dealing with this problem. Let's figure out ways to make it better."*

Paraphrase - Summarize the main point of what was shared to show understanding of their meaning. This will also give the person sharing an opportunity to clarify vague, or misinterpreted information or expand their meaning.

> **Example:** *"So what you're saying is..."*

Ask open-ended questions - Ask questions that prompt additional, specific and in depth information. Make sure the questions cannot be answered with a simple "yes" or "no."

> **Example:** *"I hear what you are saying about…."*
>
> *"What changes would you want to make to…?"*

Ask specific probing questions - Ask questions that encourage the person sharing to provide more, specific details.

> **Example:** *"Tell me more about…"*

Use short verbal affirmations. Short, positive non-judgmental statements will help the person sharing feel more comfortable in continuing sharing.

> **Example:** *"I can understand why you feel that way." "I see." "Yes, that makes sense."*

Active listening skills: Non-verbal

Nod - A few small nods show understanding of what is being said. A nod is a helpful, supportive cue, and doesn't necessarily communicate that you agree with the person sharing.

Smile. Like a nod, a small smile is encouraging: a smile can help to diffuse any tension and ensure the person sharing feels comfortable.

Avoid distracted movements - Avoid movements like glancing at your watch or phone, audibly sighing, doodling, or tapping a pen. This can make the person sharing feel frustrated and uncomfortable.

Maintain eye contact - Keep your eyes on the person sharing. However, keep it natural so as not to appear 'creepy'!

Sit with them- Be at the same eye level as the person you are talking to.

Avoid Distractions- put your cell phone away!

Motivational Interviewing (MI)

Motivational interviewing (MI) is a technique that is used by the listener to help the person in the change process resolve the ambivalence that prevents them from realizing personal goals. MI builds on Carl Rogers' optimistic and humanistic theories about people's capacity for exercising free choice and changing through a process of self-actualization. Your use of motivational interviewing is directive and intentional to elicit self-motivational statements and behavioral change from the person exploring change. This is done by creating discrepancy to enhance motivation for positive change.

Rollnick et. al. (2008) produced the acronym "RULE." We have modified their guiding principles of motivational interviewing for the relevance of pastoral care:

RULE

- **R**esist the righting reflex: People who help many times have a powerful desire to fix things, set things right, to heal people, to prevent harm and promote well-being. This is called the "Righting Reflex." Recognize the person moving towards change and healing as a primary resource in finding answers and solutions. *No one can ever change another person; only they can change themselves with God's help!*

- **U**nderstand and explore the person's own values and motivations: The person looking for solutions rather than the listener should present the arguments for change. Change is motivated through wrestling with the discrepancy between present behavior and important personal values and goals.

- **L**isten with empathy: Expressing empathy towards the person we are listening to demonstrates non-judgmental acceptance and increases the opportunity to develop trust. Acceptance enhances self-esteem and facilitates change. Skillful reflective listening is key.

- **E**mpower the person sharing, encouraging hope and optimism: Self-efficacy (self-empowerment) is important in helping them to make a change in their life.   When exploring issues, one might encounter, if the person moving towards change believes they have the ability, the likelihood of change increases. The person sharing, not the person providing pastoral care is responsible for choosing change and carrying it out. One must believe before they can achieve.

Remember that along with active listening, we want to ask good powerful open-ended (Motivational Interviewing) questions. These are in direct relation to what the person sharing is talking about, not what we think might be a good path due to a bias we have. Ask questions with a sense of empathetic curiosity without judgement.

Many times, good questions start with the following:

Explain to me…

Tell me more about…

Why do you think/feel….

Help me understand…

What might the next step look like?

If you take this action, describe to me what you think the pros and cons might be.

Why do you think unbiased, active listening and motivational interviewing is so effective while providing pastoral care?

_____
_____
_____
_____
_____
_____
_____
_____
_____
_____
_____
_____
_____

For where two or three are gathered together in my name,

I am there among them.

Matthew 18:20

Prayer

The Power of Prayer in Pastoral Care

Prayer is an essential part of providing pastoral care. It is not just a ritualistic practice, but a powerful way to connect the person receiving care to God's love, comfort, and guidance during their time of need. Prayer reminds us that we are never alone in our struggles – God is always present with us.

As pastoral care providers, we can use prayer to:

- Invite God's loving presence into the conversation.

- Affirm the worth and dignity of the person we are caring for.

- Lift their specific situation, feelings, and needs to God.

- Seek wisdom, strength, and guidance for the journey ahead.

- Reinforce the message of God's unconditional love and desire to support them.

When praying with someone, be sure to:

- Ask permission and invite them to join you in prayer.

- Keep the prayer relatively brief and focused on their expressed needs.

- Use language that is comfortable and authentic for you and them.

- Allow space for the other person to add their own prayer if they wish.

- Close with a few moments of silent reflection to listen for God's "still small voice."

The overall purpose in praying an authentic, heartfelt way that conveys God's loving presence is to connect it to the needs and concerns raised in the caring conversation. When we pray with and for others, we join our spirit with theirs and with God's Spirit in a profound way. Prayer has the power to change lives by opening us up to experience divine love during life's struggles. As pastoral caregivers, it is not only our privilege but our calling to usher in God's presence through Spirit led, compassionate prayer.

CARE

Connect – Begin by connecting with God presence and love. "Gracious God, thank you for your constant presence and care in our lives. We come before you now, trusting in your goodness and mercy."

Affirm – Affirm God's specific and relevant attributes that relate to the person's situation. "You are our refuge and strength, a very present help in times of trouble. Your love never fails, and your grace is sufficient for every need."

Requests – Lift up specific requests based on what the person has shared and align with God's will. "We ask for your healing touch upon [name]'s body, mind, and spirit. Grant them your peace that surpasses understanding. Give them wisdom and discernment as they face important decisions."

Entrust – Close by entrusting the person and their situation into God's capable hands. "We release [name] into your care, knowing that you can do immeasurably more than we could ask or imagine. We trust in your perfect plan and timing. In Jesus' mighty name we pray, Amen."

The CARE model offers prayers that bring God's presence and power to bear in the context of pastoral conversations by that connecting the person's unique situation with God's character, bringing their needs before God's throne of grace, and reaffirming trust in God's loving sovereignty over their lives.

Prayer serves as a means of connecting with God, seeking guidance, expressing gratitude, and fostering spiritual growth. Through prayer, we deepen their relationship with God and engage in the ongoing dialogue of faith. It provides a sacred space for seeking divine guidance in navigating life's complexities, whether in times of gratitude, uncertainty, or a point of decision-making. Prayer is a reminder of our reliance on God, and it plays a transformative role in fostering spiritual growth and development. Through the practice of prayer, individuals are invited into a deeper intimacy with God, where they can cultivate a profound awareness of His presence in their lives. It is not about our own skills or knowledge; we depend on the Spirit of God to work in the hearts of those we walk with.

Encourage those you are providing pastoral care to pray; together, think through specific things to pray for as this can foster a shared spiritual connection.

After listening to your classmate, write a prayer you will pray with them.

_____
_____
_____
_____
_____
_____
_____
_____
_____
_____
_____
_____

How did this exercise make you feel?

_____
_____
_____
_____
_____
_____
_____
_____
_____

Beloved, let us love one another, because love is from God; everyone who loves is born of God and knows God.
Whoever does not love does not know God,
for God is love.

1 John 4: 7-8

Thank you for spending time learning how to Listen with Love. Your facilitator will share the ending survey and certificate link.

If you found this class beneficial, please consider leaving feedback on Amazon.

Thank you and may God Bless you always!

This program was created in conjunction with and as a project for the Diocesan Church Development Institute (DCDI).

Special thanks to the Rev. Elisabeth Tunney, the Rev. Kevin Morris and the Rev. Karen Davis-Lawson and the Episcopal Diocese of Long Island for the opportunity to help us grow in Christ.

References

Greenstein, L. (2017). 9 ways to fight mental health stigma. *NAMI*. Paragraph 2. Retrieved on December 30, 2020 from https://www.nami.org/blogs/nami-blog/october-2017/9-ways-to-fight-mental-health-stigma

Loftquist, W. A. (1989). A leadership development program. *Associates for Youth Development, Inc.* Pages 29-41.

Marriam-Webster (n.d.). Bias. In *Merriam-Webster.com dictionary*. Retrieved December 28, 2020, from https://www.merriam-webster.com/dictionary/bias

Merriam-Webster (n.d.). Stigma. In *Merriam-Webster.com dictionary*. Retrieved December 30, 2020, from https://www.merriam-webster.com/dictionary/stigma

New Revised Standard Version, (2021) Updated Edition. National Council of Churches of Christ in the United States of America.

Psychology Today (2020). Bias. *Sussex Publishers, LLC.* Retrieved December 28, 2020 from https://www.psychologytoday.com/us/basics/bias

Rollnick, Miller, & Buttler (2008). Motivational interviewing in health care. Helping patients change behavior. New York, NY: *Guilford Press.*

White, W. L. (n.d.). The rhetoric of recovery advocacy: an essay on the power of language. Page 2. Retrieved on December 30, 2020 from http://www.williamwhitepapers.com/pr/2001RhetoricofRecoveryAdvocacy.pdf

Notes

www.ingramcontent.com/pod-product-compliance
Lightning Source LLC
Chambersburg PA
CBHW081644040426
42449CB00015B/3449